Birth of a Stork

Birth of a Stork

Heiderose and Andreas Fischer-Nagel

Translated by Noel Simon

J.M. Dent & Sons Ltd
London & Melbourne

First published in Great Britain 1985

Originally published in German under the title
Das Storchenjahr

Printed in Germany
This book is phototypeset in Itek Century Schoolbook
by Copyright, London W1.

British Library Cataloguing in Publication Data

Fischer-Nagel, Andreas
Birth of a stork.
1. Storks—Juvenile literature
I. Title II. Fischer-Nagel, Heiderose
III. Das Storchenjahr. *English*
598′.34 QL696.C535

ISBN 0-460-06187-9

There cannot be many people who still believe the old wives' tale that the stork is responsible for bringing babies into the world. Nor, sad to say, can there be many with even a slight knowledge of the European white stork's way of life. This large bird with spindly, red, stilt-like legs, long, red, pointed bill and black-and-white plumage was at one time common; but nowadays more people will be familiar with it through fables than will actually have seen one in the wild. The stork is in fact a woodland dweller, but in some places builds its nest on the roofs and chimneys of houses. It has long been considered a symbol of fertility, and the traditional belief that it brings good luck still holds good to the extent that many people build special platforms on their roofs in the hope that storks will nest on them.

Unfortunately the stork is becoming increasingly rare, largely because those parts of Europe where it lives – from Holland to western Russia – no longer have enough of its special food – frogs, small fish, pond snails, and the like. Most of the ponds and marshes which provide a suitable habitat for frogs have disappeared. Another factor is the numerous electricity pylons and high tension cables criss-crossing the countryside. Storks flying into them are likely to be injured or killed. Factory chimneys belching forth poisonous gases are yet another source of danger.

Like many birds – the swallow, for example – the stork is a migratory species. This means that it spends the summer in Europe, where it nests and raises its young. But as winter approaches it flies south where the climate is warmer and food more plentiful. Each species of bird has its own particular wintering ground to which it returns every year. The European stork winters in Africa.

In order to know how best to protect this splendid bird we must learn more about its habits and special needs and in this way come to understand it better.

From the middle of March, when it is spring in Europe, the white storks leave their winter quarters in Africa on their return migration. The males are almost always the first to arrive. After a long flight of more than 10,000 km they land with uncanny accuracy in the very colony they had left the previous autumn. No sooner have they landed than each concentrates on occupying and holding a nest, sometimes in the face of strong competition. Successful males make the loud bill-clacking noise known as 'clappering'. This proclaims that they own the nests.

The females follow a few days later. They return to the very nests they had used the previous year, for female storks 'pair' with a particular nest, not a particular male. Each female accepts whatever male happens to be occupying her nest, whether or not he is her mate of the previous season. Pairs of birds dance excitedly on their nests. Without further ado the pair starts putting the future stork nursery into good order. Repairs are carried out by collecting great quantities of twigs and sticks to patch up the nest. The same nests are used year

after year. Over a period of several years they become so bulky and heavy that in autumn, when the storks have once again flown south, the householders have to reduce them in size or prop them up with supports. Some people instal special platforms on their roofs on which the storks can build nests. Sometimes old cartwheels are used for this purpose. This is done partly to attract the storks and partly to protect their roofs and chimneys which could be damaged by the weight of the nests.

While the nests are being built, as well as for some time after, each pair of storks has to keep a careful watch on its neighbours. At the slightest opportunity they will try to steal nesting material. Some even look for unoccupied nests which they can take over. A ready-made nest saves them the trouble of having to make one themselves. It is therefore necessary for one or other of the pair always to remain on the nest while the other gathers nesting material. Even this precaution does not altogether prevent their nests being robbed, and this often leads to a great deal of fighting. Inevitably it sometimes happens that eggs which have already been laid are pushed out of the nest and crash to the ground.

After rebuilding the framework of the nest the storks line it with grass cuttings, hay, moss, feathers and other materials – sometimes even plastic bags. They work very hard at making the nest strong and comfortable. Occasionally they pause to mate so that the female will lay fertile eggs in which the embryos will develop.

As soon as nest building is finished the female lays her first egg in it.

The eggs are pure white and slightly shiny, and about the same size as those shown in the photograph. Every two days the female lays another egg. Altogether she will lay a total of two to five eggs. After laying the second she starts to brood. Lowering herself gently on to the clutch of eggs she covers them with her plumage to keep them warm. The eggs take thirty-three days to hatch. Both parents help incubate the eggs and care for the young.

After thirty-three days the first chick appears. The first sign is when a tiny hole appears in the eggshell. Gradually it becomes bigger until a large crack appears at the blunt end of the egg. With its sharp egg-tooth – a tiny, horny growth on the upper part of the bill which disappears a few days after birth – the chick breaks through the eggshell. Again and again the tiny bird tries to get out. A little foot is the first thing to appear, then the whole bill, and then a wing. After that the chick rests awhile as the birth is an exhausting process. At the next attempt his head breaks through the eggshell.

He has done it! Tired and exhausted the newly hatched chick flops on to the floor of the nest. His head looks far too big for his scraggy neck, and his head feathers are still wet. His bill is neither long nor red like the older storks. It is hard to imagine how this tiny bundle of fluff could ever become a large stork.

At last everything is done. The eggshell lies in two pieces close to the tiny chick. His body looks podgy and shapeless. A newborn stork weighs about 65-80 grams, as much as two chicken eggs. His first fine down – or downy feathers –remain stuck together. His eyes are still shut. But they soon open.

Now the adults start brooding their young. Very carefully, the mother bird lowers herself on to the newborn chick, warming and drying it.

Normally there is an interval of a day between births. The oldest chick is quite well grown by the time the last egg hatches. Unfortunately not all the young will survive. Some are too frail at birth, and as there is seldom sufficient food to go round the younger chicks often die of starvation.

The adult birds bring only small prey for their chicks to eat – earthworms, beetles, grasshoppers and other insects – which they find in nearby fields and watermeadows. The little storks thrive on this diet and grow very quickly.

Only one day after being hatched the little stork's appearance is already beginning to improve. His white, downy feathers have dried, and he can also hold up his heavy head for short periods. Comparing the day-old chick with the egg, it is difficult to imagine how he could possibly have fitted inside.

During the next few days the little stork grows very quickly; but these first days of life are also the most dangerous. Cold, wet weather can turn the nest into

a deadly quagmire. And lurking in the background are numerous crows waiting only for an unguarded moment to seize a chick. The sun, too, can be harmful if the chicks are exposed to its full glare. This is why one of the adults takes care always to guard the nest and shade the young birds from the sun. Not until the chicks are large enough to need a great deal of food do the parent birds leave the nest for long periods.

Although most people are fond of the stork, they have in recent years been largely responsible for making its survival in Europe increasingly difficult. Each year fewer and fewer storks return from Africa. Houses now stand where previously there were open fields and water-meadows; marshes, and the streams which fed them, have been drained for agricultural purposes. The stork can no longer find enough food. A high proportion of the nestlings is sure to die; at best only one or two leave each nest as full-grown birds.

As long as there are habitats as ideal as the one shown in this photograph storks will have everything they need. In such perfect surroundings they will always find enough food: frogs, tadpoles, waterbeetles, fish, pond snails and much more. But without adequate protection the stork cannot survive. It is a long way to Africa and the flight is beset with dangers: some birds are shot or trapped by hunters; others die from eating poisoned locusts.

As you already know, the white stork catches frogs. But it does not live on them exclusively.

With head held high, a stork strides slowly through the grass on long legs. Suddenly it lunges forward, seizing a grasshopper, a mouse, or even a snake in its long, sharp bill.

Like other birds, storks have a crop, or pouch, in which they store food which is later regurgitated to feed their young. Having filled its crop with a variety of food, the adult stork flies back to its nest where the chicks wait, ravenously hungry.

If the bird is not feeding its young the food passes from the crop into its own stomach.

Some of the prey species are photographed on the right: at the top is a frog; in the centre a grass snake; and, below, a grasshopper.

In heavy rain the normally white nestlings soon become a dirty grey, smeared with dirt from the bottom of the nest. One of the parent birds then squats close to the chicks to warm and dry them. You can see from the photograph on the right how tiny a baby stork is.

While one of the parent birds searches for food its mate spends the time on watch preening its feathers. Clean plumage is extremely important, indeed vitally necessary, for all birds. Each individual feather is drawn through the bill, cleaned and carefully restored to its place. A foot is used to groom any parts that the bill cannot reach.

Young storks grow at a tremendous rate. The day soon arrives when they have to be ringed. A man from the bird-ringing station – a scientific institute for the protection of bird life – climbs up to the storks' nest. He places a large, but light, metal ring, marked with a number and the name of the bird-ringing station, on one leg and clips it into position with a special pair of pliers. From then on, wherever the stork goes, whether it is caught or found dead, its origins can be traced. The scientists can then work out how far the bird has flown, how long it has taken on the journey, and perhaps the actual route it took to its winter quarters. As well as recording their exact age, these rings offer the only way of knowing for sure where and when the storks winter in Africa.

Within a few weeks the young storks have grown large enough to stand up in the nest or, like the pair in the left-hand photograph, to squat on their shanks –the lower part of the leg. Their feathers now match those of the adults very closely. All their pinion feathers are black, while the remaining feathers are pure white. Their parents leave them for longer periods. Dozing peacefully, the two young storks in the right-hand photograph sit waiting to be fed.

Before it is ready to fly a stork must exercise its wings. It does so by constantly spreading and stretching them; every newly-grown feather will be given lengthy and careful grooming. With the help of grease secreted from a special gland beneath the tail, the bird keeps its feathers supple and waterproof.

At the age of about two months an important moment comes for the young stork. He is finally 'fledged'. Facing into wind, he spreads his wings and takes his first flight. Flying to the next chimney he is still a little unsteady as he stands on the unfamiliar, smooth surface. Time and again young storks fall off such chimneys, but usually they come to no harm. Helpful people place them back on the roof, from which they try ever more ambitious flights.

If the white stork is not to disappear completely from Europe's native fauna it is essential that people take the trouble to help it. If bad weather threatens to kill the young nestlings from wet or cold immediate action must be taken. This is the reason why ornithologists constantly check the number of nests and the nestlings in them. Any that are in danger are brought to the bird stations, examined, given suitable food and generally cared for. Sometimes a newly hatched chick is brought in. It often happens that parent birds cannot manage to hatch the eggs as well as feed the chicks. In searching for food they have constantly to be away from the nest. And when that happens the eggs and young are left unprotected. These circumstances justify taking the eggs away and hatching them in an incubator.

The raising of a newly hatched stork is difficult as it requires so much attention. By providing the best opportunities for study, bird stations specializing in the care and protection of storks make it possible for us to know more about the bird's natural history. The stork's habit of nesting on houses has also made it easier to study it at close quarters and over long periods of time.

Alert and intelligent, the white stork stalks the fields and water-meadows searching for frogs, mice and other creatures. Often it stops abruptly, with one leg raised in the air and its head inclined to one side, as it listens and watches attentively. Suddenly it lunges. With faultless precision the stork catches something and gulps it down.

In this picture you can clearly see the metal ring on its left leg.

Here is an impression of a stork's footprint in the sand.

Storks are found all over the world, but only two species live in Europe. Apart from the white stork, which occurs from Holland and Spain across northern Europe into Russia and Asia Minor, the only other is the very shy and even rarer black stork (in the large photograph on the right), which is found from northern Germany through eastern Europe into parts of Asia. Altogether, there are fifteen other species, among them the African saddlebill (in the left-hand picture above) and the black-necked stork (above right). Both are much larger than the white stork.

By August, the last of the young storks will have learned to fly. After each flight they return to the nest, and during the next fortnight will continue to be fed by their parents. Soon, though, they must learn to live without their parents' help. They begin to show signs of restlessness. On the ground they assemble together in ever larger groups, while in the sky they circle higher and higher until they almost disappear from sight. One day they fail to return: their first migratory flight to Africa has begun. With help from the sun and an instinctive knowledge of the course they must follow, they fly on an accurate compass bearing. Normally the adults take the lead: with their knowledge and experience of the flyway they are familiar with the correct route. These long migratory flights, from one hemisphere to the other, are one of the wonders of nature.

In contrast with the European summer, filled with the sound of clappering, the autumn seems very quiet after the storks' departure. Those who are fortunate enough to live in countries where there are storks always look forward to the coming spring and to hearing reports that these splendid birds are on their way back. But to make sure that the white stork continues to return each year, people must do all they can to see that its habitat is properly conserved.